NORTHERN ARGYLL

A pictorial souvenir

NESS PUBLISHING

2 At the westernmost tip of the Isle of Mull lies Fionnphort, from where it is a short ferry crossing to the sacred Isle of Iona, seen in the distance.

NORTHERN ARGYLL

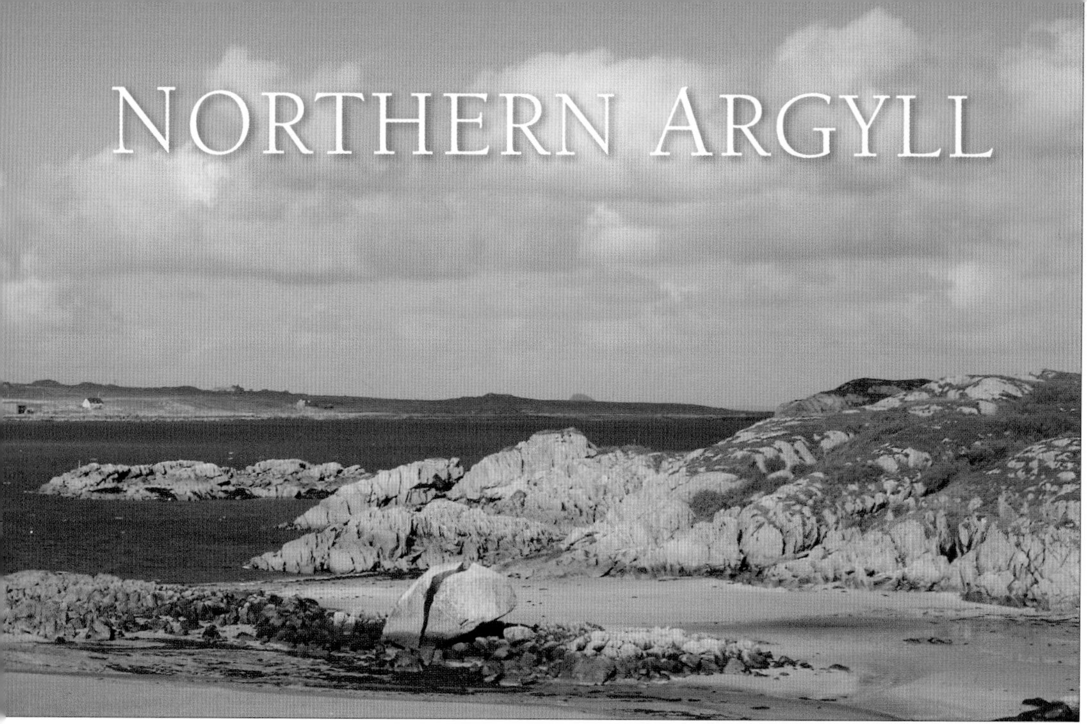

Introduction: welcome to Argyll!

This magnificent realm of land and water stretches approximately 120 miles up Scotland's western seaboard, incorporates 26 inhabited islands and is a hotbed of ancient history. Its geographical range encompasses some of Scotland's highest mountains, its longest inland loch and a coastline that is in part reminiscent of the Mediterranean and at times battered and shaped by the ferocity of the Atlantic storms that frequently assail it. Its many sea lochs and islands make Argyll's coastline longer than that of France; its landmass of 6,930 sq. km. makes it larger than Belgium.

The name 'Argyll' comes from the Gaelic *Earra-Ghaidheal* meaning the boundary of the Gaels. It was indeed frontier territory, for the Gaels, a people of Celtic ethnicity who migrated from Ireland, inevitably found other peoples already established. Nevertheless, by about 500AD they were able to establish the kingdom of Dál Riata in Argyll. This name was taken from that which already applied to a kingdom based on present-day County Antrim in Northern Ireland, with the seat of kingship being moved to Dunadd in Argyll around this time.

It should be pointed out that Argyll was once more extensive than its present northern boundary indicates, as it formerly held Glen Coe, Ardgour and Ardnamurchan. However, these areas have also belonged to the district of Lochaber which lies to the north of Argyll, so they have been included in

From the summit of Bidean nam Bian (1150m/3773ft), Glen Coe, the view south down Loch Etive leads the eye into northern Argyll.

the book of that title in this series. But as a nod to the region's past, the picture on page 5 shows the view south into Glen Etive from Bidean nam Bian, once the highest point in Argyll.

Celtic Christianity came to Scotland as a result of the missionary work of St Columba (521–597) and those who followed him. He established a monastery on the Isle of Iona in 563AD. In the 12th century a Benedictine abbey and nunnery were founded there, which remained the principal religious houses of the Isles until the Scottish Reformation from 1560. As the cradle of Christianity in Scotland and through the ongoing ministry of the Iona Community, Iona remains a major focus of Christian pilgrimage in Scotland, a sacred site which draws people from all over the world.

As the title indicates, this book concentrates on the northern half of Argyll because the territory as a whole is too large to be adequately covered in one volume (the southern half of Argyll will be covered in a subsequent book in this series). Starting in the north, it works its way down through the modern-day county of Argyll and Bute in zigzag fashion with the aim of illustrating as many as possible of the principal places of interest. These are wide-ranging so as to show the great variety of sights and experiences to be found in the area. After east-west meanderings, including

The St Margaret window, Iona Abbey.

the islands of Mull and Iona, we shall travel as far south as Kilmartin, the heart of one of Scotland's richest archaeological landscapes, where there are over 350 archaeological and historical monuments within a six-mile radius. Many of these are of national importance, some of international importance, and many more of regional significance. The Prehistoric centre of the region is Kilmartin Glen, with its standing stones, burial cairns, rock art, forts, duns and carved stones.

But now, let this pictorial tour remind you of or prepare you for the best that this impressive land has to show. Whether your interest lies in trekking up mountains like Ben Cruachan or Ben More, soaking up the splendour of castles such as Kilchurn or Inveraray, delving into the misty past or walking in moody glens, let the exploration begin!

Model of a Sunderland flying boat at Oban's War and Peace Museum.

8 A tranquil scene at the southern end of Loch Etive near Ardchattan, in the Benderloch district of Argyll. See also p.19.

10 From the southern slopes of the Glen Coe mountains, a view into upper Glen Etive with Ben Starav rising dramatically from the valley floor.

The head of Loch Etive. From here it is 17 miles to the loch's outflow to the sea at Connel. Ben Cruachan can be seen in the distance . . .

12 . . . and when studied in close-up, the fearsome aspect of its summit ridge can be seen to good effect. At 1126m/3694ft it is Scotland's 31st-highest mountain.

To the west of Ben Cruachan, between Taynuilt and Connel on the southern shores of Loch Etive, the beautiful Achnacloich Garden shows off its spring colours.

14 Castle Stalker stands on an islet on the edge of Loch Linnhe near the village of Portnacroish. It dates back to the 15th century and was the traditional stronghold of the Stewarts of Appin.

From near Castle Stalker, this view looks across Loch Linnhe to the northern end of the island of Lismore. About nine miles long, narrow, low-lying and fertile, it has a population of about 180.

16 A spring view of the village of Port Appin, from where the passenger ferry to Lismore takes about five minutes to reach the island. Lismore's north lighthouse can be seen in the distance.

To the east of Port Appin, the main road (A828) along the coast crosses Loch Creran (a sea loch), from where this easterly view captures Ben Sgulaird in the distance.

18 Otters (left) and a baby seal at the Sea Life Sanctuary located near Barcaldine on the shores of Loch Creran, a few miles north of Oban.

The remains of Ardchattan Priory, located near the scene on pages 8-9. It was founded by the strict Valliscaulian order in 1231. Inset: Architectural detail at Ardchattan.

20 Continuing south along the coast we come to Connel Bridge. This used to serve both road and rail but the railway branch line from Connel to Ballachulish closed in the 1960s.

Looking inland (east) from Connel Bridge, which crosses the outflow of Loch Etive.
At high tide the water is calm but at low tide the Falls of Lora appear as the sea recedes.

22 Located near Taynuilt on the southern shore of Loch Etive, Bonawe Iron Furnace is the most complete charcoal-fuelled ironworks in Britain – a fascinating place to visit (Historic Scotland).

Raw materials were landed and Bonawe's pig iron despatched from Lorn Quay on Loch Etive, which still survives to the left of this picture. The Glen Coe mountains are in the distance.

24 Eastwards from Taynuilt and through the Pass of Brander, we arrive at Loch Awe. This panorama shows Kilchurn Castle on the lochside to the left and Ben Eunaich snow-capped on the right.

26 Ben Cruachan rises from the head of Loch Awe and gives hill walkers a tough climb. But views like this are the reward! Here we look north up Glen Etive towards the Glen Coe mountains.

The eastward view along Cruachan's granite ridge towards Ben Diamh, at 998m/3274ft also a Munro (Scottish mountains above 914m/3000ft). Compare this picture with the one on p.12.

28 Kilchurn Castle, built by Sir Colin Campbell of Glenorchy c.1550. Much enlarged in 1693, it incorporates the first purpose-built barracks in Scotland. Open to visitors in summer (Historic Scotland).

We now turn north-west and travel up Glen Orchy, through which the picturesque River Orchy tumbles over many waterfalls such at this one at Allt Broighleachan, a site of special scientific interest (SSSI).

30 At the northern end of Glen Orchy, the beautifully conical shape of Beinn Dorain (1076m/3530ft) greets the eye. The level line at its base is the Glasgow to Fort William railway.

We are now in the most north-easterly corner of present-day Argyll.
A few miles north of Ben Dorain is Loch Tulla, seen at the dawn of a winter's day.

32 Returning now to Loch Awe: at 41km/25miles, it is Scotland's longest inland loch. This view scans its northern reaches from the grounds of the Ardanaiseig Hotel.

A few miles to the south and on the western shore of Loch Awe, an opportunity to explore the loch is presented at the jetty of the Taychreggan Hotel.

34 Only the area around Kilchrenan remains sunlit while the darkness gathers as a storm approaches Loch Awe.

And as the rain falls, a rainbow adds its luminescence to the scene.

36 Back by the coast near Connel, Dunstaffnage Castle was built by 1275 on a huge rock overlooking the Firth of Lorn and provided the MacDougalls with a mighty stronghold (Historic Scotland).

In the trees close to the castle is Dunstaffnage Chapel, built in the 13th century. The remains of the paired windows in the chancel show a high standard of workmanship (Historic Scotland).

38 About three miles south of Dunstaffnage we come to Oban, the principal town of northern Argyll and a major port for ferries to the Hebrides. In this evening scene, the Mull ferry arrives.

Evening shadows in McCaig's Tower, Oban. John Stuart McCaig built it during the winters of 1895 to 1902 to provide work for stonemasons who were otherwise unemployed at this time of year.

40 The vantage point of Pulpit Hill, Oban, is a good place to watch the sun setting over the Sound of Mull, with the island of Kerrera silhouetted against the sea.

42 A garden of remembrance in Oban with Dunollie Castle beyond. The first record of a fort on this site goes right back to 686. The present ruin is thought to date from the 12th century.

Oban (meaning 'little bay' in Gaelic) is a popular resort that grew rapidly after the arrival of the railway from Glasgow, although it had a steamship connection from there since 1812.

44 Looking down from McCaig's Tower (floodlit towards the right of the cover picture) is a good place to appreciate Oban's maritime setting and the pattern of islands through which the ferries have to navigate.

Vibrant spring colours enhance this picture of Oban's western fringe, with Kerrera and Mull beyond.

46 The Isle of Kerrera is set in the mouth of Oban Bay, acting as a natural breakwater for the harbour. Sunderland flying boats (see p.7) were based here during the Second World War.

No visit to Oban is complete without an exploration of lovely Glen Lonan to the east of the town. This pastoral scene, complete with mountain backdrop, sums it up.

48 And so to Mull. Approaching the island by the ferry from Oban gives a good idea of the contrasts that await. Perched on its rocky promontory, Duart Castle stands guard over the surrounding waters.

Duart Castle has been the base of the Clan Maclean's sea-borne power for over 400 years.
It is part of a chain of castles up the Sound of Mull to Mingary Castle in Ardnamurchan.

50 This is the view from near Duart Castle across Duart Bay towards the mountainous hinterland of Mull.

Since 1984 the Mull & West Highland Narrow Gauge Railway has transported thousands of visitors over the 1.25 miles from Craignure (near the ferry port) to Torosay Castle.

52 Torosay Castle was completed in 1858 by the eminent architect David Bryce in the Scottish Baronial style. The statues came from a deserted villa in Padua, Italy.

The Castle is surrounded by magnificent gardens. This is the Fountain Terrace with its view out to sea.

54 Journeying west through Mull soon brings about a change of scenery as the road threads through Glen More, from where the chiselled outline of Ben More, Mull's highest hill, comes into view.

Red deer are plentiful on Mull. This stag has a fine set of 10-point antlers.

56 Taking the north-westerly route along the coast from Craignure brings us to the village of Salen. Amongst the sights here are the retired boats on the left.

Aros Castle, a stone 13th-century hall house and courtyard fortress built by the MacDonalds, can just be made out in the centre distance.

58 10 miles on from Salen in the north of Mull is Tobermory. It is a picture-postcard of a place with many brightly painted buildings along the main street.

Tobermory was built as a fishing port in the late 18th century and is now the main village on Mull. It is home to many places of interest including the Tobermory Distillery.

60 Local businesses also provide wildlife-watching excursions including boat trips to see dolphins, seals and seabirds. This is an evening view of Tobermory Bay.

Tobermory derives its name from the Gaelic 'Tobar Mhoire' meaning the Well of Mary.
The village looks as attractive by night as it does by day.

62 West of Tobermory near the pretty village of Dervaig is the Old Byre Heritage Centre, a must for anyone who wants to absorb the history of Mull. This is a model of an early monastic settlement.

Mull boasts many fine beaches such as this one at Calgary Bay, a little further round the northern coast.

64 Mull is an island of many waterfalls. Some plunge straight into the sea, like Eas Fors, seen on the left from across Loch Tuath with the view from the top on the right.

A number of smaller islands lie off Mull's coast, such as Ulva, seen in the distance. The islet-strewn narrows in the foreground are near the hamlet of Oskamull, where Loch Tuath meets Loch na Keal.

66 The winding road around Loch na Keal offers many fine sights, such as this one across to the little island of Inch Kenneth, where the rocky outcrops contrast with the boulders in the foreground.

The next sea loch to the south is Loch Scridain. Across the water on its northern shore the mountains of Mull beckon. Ben More (966m/3169ft) is seen again, this time with its head in the clouds. 67

68 Moving further west along the Ross of Mull, from near the village of Bunessan we see this impressive formation which is a typical feature of the island's geology. Across the sea from here is . . .

. . . the tiny island of Staffa, famous for its columnar basalt formations and Fingal's Cave, seen here.
This was the inspiration for Felix Mendelssohn's Hebrides Overture.

70 Having reached Fionnphort (see pages 2-3) and crossed to Iona, we come first to the Iona Nunnery. The ruins have the air of a garden thanks to the many flowers grown there.

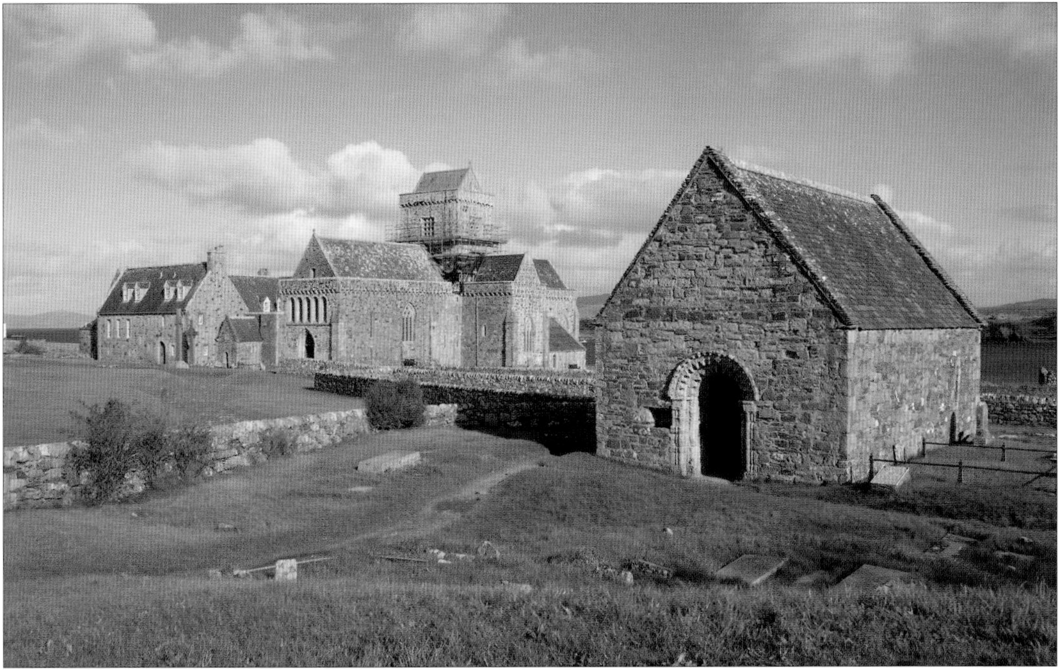

For the pilgrim this is journey's end. On the right is St Oran's Chapel, Iona's oldest surviving ecclesiastical building. To the left is Iona Abbey, a place of worship for people from all over the world.

72 From left to right, St John's Cross (replica), St Columba's shrine and, in front of the doorway of the Abbey Church, the well. Two members of the Iona Community pass the time of day.

From the ferry slipway at Baile Mor, Iona's village, inviting rock pools wait to be investigated.

74 Leaving Mull and travelling south, the next island is Seil. But Seil, on the left, is only separated from the mainland on the right by the narrowest sliver of sea, spanned by the 'Bridge over the Atlantic'.

On the right at the foot of the cliff is the village of Easdale, Seil and on the left the island that is also named Easdale. Once famed for their slate, they were known as the 'Islands that Roofed the World'.

Left: here, from Craobh Haven on the mainland are the tips of two more islands, Shuna and Luing (upper right) while in the distance are Scarba (right) and Jura (left). Above: in the Gulf of Corryvreckan between Scarba and Jura, the combination of an underwater rock pinnacle and certain sea conditions produce turbulence that creates a whirlpool, or standing waves several feet high as in this picture.

Craobh Haven is near the mouth of Loch Melfort, the head of which is seen here, looking inland towards the village of Kilmelford. The National Trust for Scotland's Arduaine Garden is nearby.

78 Continuing south and taking a small detour east towards the village of Ford, we come to this jewel of a scene at tiny Loch Ederline.

Rejoining the main road (A816) as it sweeps down into Kilmartin Glen reveals 16th-century Carnasserie Castle (Historic Scotland) on the hillside to the west of the road.

80 The Kilmartin area is rich in ancient sites and artefacts. Left: carving on the rear of an early stone crucifix in Kilmartin Church. Right: reconstruction of a hermit's cell at Kilmartin House Museum.

Nether Largie south cairn: this is the only chambered cairn of the five in Kilmartin's 2km-long linear cemetery. Excavations in 1864 revealed evidence for use over perhaps a thousand years.

82 Just 200 metres away are Temple Wood stone circles, the southern of which is above. They date back to at least 3,000 BC, the northern circle being built first and then apparently replaced by the southern.

A short distance further south are the Ballymeanoch standing stones, comprising two roughly parallel rows – the nearer pair and the line of four framed between them.

84 We now flit about 30 miles north-west to the Arrochar Alps, a range of mountains between Inveraray and Loch Lomond. Here we see Ben Vorlich (943m/3094ft) rising above Loch Lomond.

It may not be so high at 884m/2900ft, but Ben Arthur, usually known as The Cobbler, is the most distinctive mountain in the Arrochar Alps. It stands above the village of Arrochar.

86 Having left the Arrochar Alps (see top right of this picture), we have come round the head of Loch Fyne to the beautiful town of Inveraray, seen here from the top of The Duke's Tower.

Inveraray Castle is a remarkable and unique piece of architecture incorporating Baroque, Palladian and Gothic styles. It took over 40 years to build, from 1746 to 1789.

88 The classic view of 'new' Inveraray, the planned town built from 1743 to replace the original village that was demolished to make way for the castle. The white buildings line Front Street.

The Duke's Tower is to the right – it houses what is said to be the second heaviest peal of bells in the world.

90 And now the view from Front Street looking over to where the previous picture was taken. The hill rising behind the bridge over the River Aray is Duniquaich.

Moored at the town pier is the *Arctic Penguin*, a triple-masted iron schooner built in Dublin in 1910. It is home to the Inveraray Maritime Heritage Museum. Behind is the 'puffer' *The Vital Spark*.

92 Inveraray Jail is another first-class attraction, offering an interactive experience of life in a 19th-century prison. Here, in the courtroom, the trial continues!

South-west of Inveraray is Auchindrain, a restored highland township. The conserved buildings have been furnished and equipped, presenting a fascinating glimpse into highland life in the past.

94 A few miles further on are Crarae Gardens, on the shores of Loch Fyne. Trees and shrubs from all over the temperate world thrive here (National Trust for Scotland).

We end our tour with a look down onto the town of Lochgilphead, administrative headquarters of Argyll. It is just into southern Argyll, so we shall return for a closer look in another book…

Published 2010 by Ness Publishing, 47 Academy Street, Elgin, Moray, IV30 1LR
Phone/fax 01343 549663 www.nesspublishing.co.uk

ISBN 978-1-906549-11-4

Front cover: Oban; p.1: Rowan trees at Ardchattan; p.4: in Inveraray; this page: St John's Cross, Iona; back cover: Loch Lomond.

For a list of websites and phone numbers please turn over >